CENGAGE Learning

Novels for Students, Volume 5 Copyright Notice

Copyright © 1999

Gale Research
27500 Drake Rd.
Farmington Hills, MI 48331-3535

ISBN 0-7876-2115-3
ISSN 1094-3552

Printed in the United States of America.
1 0 9 8 7 6 5 4 3

The Color Purple

Alice Walker

1982

Introduction

The Color Purple, Alice Walker's third novel, was published in 1982. The novel brought fame and financial success to its author. It also won her considerable praise and much criticism for its controversial themes. Many reviewers were disturbed by her portrayal of black males, which they found un-duly negative. When the novel was made into a film in 1985 by Steven Spielberg, Walker became even more successful and controversial. While she was criticized for negative portrayal of her male characters, Walker was admired for her powerful portraits of black women. Reviewers praised her for her use of the epistolary form, in which written correspondence between characters comprises the content of the book, and her ability to use black folk English. Reflecting her early political interests as a civil rights worker during the 1960s, many of her social views are expressed in the novel. In *The Color Purple*, as in her other writings, Walker focuses on the theme of double repression of black women in the American experience. Walker contends that black women suffer from discrimination by the white community, and from a second repression from black males, who impose the double standard of white society on women. As the civil rights movement helped shape Ms. Walker's thinking regarding racial issues at home, it also shaped her interest in Africa. During the 1960s, a strong interest in ethnic and racial identity stimulated many African Americans to look for their roots in Africa. The primary theme of *The Color Purple*, though, reflects Walker's desire to project a positive outcome in life, even under the harshest conditions. Her central character triumphs over adversity and forgives those who oppressed her. This central theme of the triumph of good over evil is no doubt the source of the book's great success.

Author Biography

Alice Walker was born in the rural community of Eatonton, Georgia, in 1944. Most of Eatonton's residents were tenant farmers. When she was eight years old, Walker was blinded in one eye when her brother accidentally shot her with a BB gun. Having grown self-conscious as a result of her injury, Alice withdrew to writing poetry. She began her college education at Spelman in 1961 but transferred to Sarah Lawrence in 1963. After graduating in 1965, she went to Mississippi as a civil rights activist. There she met Melvyn Leventhal, a white civil rights attorney, whom she married in 1967. The Leventhals were the first legally married interracial couple to live in Jackson, Mississippi. They divorced in 1976. Alice Walker's first novel was published in 1970 and her second one in 1976. Both books dealt with the civil rights movement. *The Color Purple* was published in 1982 and brought Walker overnight success and recognition as an important American writer. In 1989 Walker published *The Temple of My Familiar*, in which she used a mythic context as a framework to cover a half million years of human history. In this work, Walker explored the social structure of a matriarchal society and the beginning of patriarchal ones. As in her other works, the author explored racial and sexual relationships. Walker's novel, *Possessing the Secret of Joy*, was published in 1992. Along with novels, Walker has written many collected short stories and books of poetry. Many of her stories have been included in anthologies. An active contributor to periodicals, Walker has had her works published in many magazines, including *Harper's, Negro Digest, Black World, Essence*, and the *Denver Quarterly*. Besides her writing career, Walker has been a teacher of black studies, a writer in residence, and a professor of literature at a number of colleges and universities. She has received numerous awards for her writing, including a National Endowment for the Arts grant, a Guggenheim Award, an O. Henry Award, an American Book Award, and the Pulitzer Prize. She has one daughter and lives in California.

Plot Summary

First Period

In *The Color Purple*, the story is told through letters. The only sentences outside the letters are the first two: "You better not never tell nobody but God. It'd kill your mammy." Silenced forever, the main character, fourteen year old Celie, writes letters to God. Her father has raped her, and she has two children, a girl and a boy, whom "Pa" took away from her. Celie's mother has died and Pa is looking too much at her little sister, Nettie.

Mr. wants to marry Nettie but Pa rejects him because of the Mr.'s scandals with Shug Avery, a blues singer. Celie manages to get a picture of Shug and falls in love with her. Eventually, Mr. agrees to take Celie instead of Nettie because Pa offers him a cow.

Once she is in his care, Mr. beats Celie all the time. Meanwhile, Nettie runs away from Pa and comes to Mr.'s house, but when she rejects him, he throws her out. Celie advises Nettie to ask her daughter Olivia's new "mother" for help. Nettie promises to write but her letters never arrive.

One day, Shug Avery comes to town, but Mr. does not take Celie to see her. Harpo, Mr.'s son, gets married to Sofia, a strong brave woman, and when he complains that Sofia does not obey him, Celie advises Harpo to beat her. Sofia finds out, and in the conversation that follows, Celie realizes she is jealous of Sofia: "You do what I can't. Fight," she says.

Second Period

Shug is ill and Mr. brings her to his home. To Celie's surprise, she calls Mr. by his first name, Albert. Celie's love and care make Shug better; Shug starts composing a new song.

Sofia finally leaves Harpo, who turns his house into a juke joint and asks Shug to sing. Shug invites Celie to the performance. Shug sings "A Good Man Is Hard to Find" and then her new piece, called "Celie's Song." Celie discovers that she is important to someone.

Before leaving, Shug says she will make sure Mr. never beats Celie again. She also teaches Celie to love herself. By the time Sofia returns with a new man and six children instead of five, Harpo has a little girlfriend he calls Squeak. Sofia and Squeak hit each other in the juke joint, and finally Sofia leaves.

The mayor's wife sees Sofia in town with the kids and asks Sofia to be her maid. Sofia answers: "Hell no" and hits the mayor when he protests. She is arrested, beaten and left in prison. Meanwhile, Squeak takes care of Sofia's children. When she finds out one of Sofia's wardens is her uncle, Squeak tries to save Sofia. She convinces the warden that working for the mayor's wife would be a better punishment for Sofia. The warden forces Squeak to have sexual intercourse with him. When Squeak goes back home, furious and humiliated, she orders Harpo to call her Mary Agnes, her real name. Sofia starts working for the mayor's wife, but she is treated as a slave.

On her next visit, Shug is married. She and Celie have missed each other, and one night, when the men are away, Celie tells Shug the story of Pa and the children. Shug kisses her, and they make love.

Third Period

One day, Shug asks Celie about Nettie, and together they realize Mr. has been hiding Nettie's letters. They finally recover them from Mr.'s trunk.

Unlike Celie's letters to God, Nettie's letters are written in standard English. The day Nettie left, Mr. followed her and tried to rape her. She fought, and he had to give up, but he promised she would never hear from Celie again. Nettie went to see Corrine, Olivia's new mother, and her husband, the Reverend Samuel. She also met Celie's other child, Adam. Samuel was a member of a Missionary Society, and Nettie decided to go to Africa with the family. First, they went to New York, where Nettie discovered Harlem and African culture. Then, they went to England and Senegal, where Nettie saw what Europe was doing to Africa: robbing its treasures, using its peoples, and impoverishing the land.

Celie reads Nettie's letters and wants to kill

Mr. for having hidden them. To help Celie control herself, Shug suggests that Celie make herself a pair of pants and go on reading the letters.

When the missionary group arrived in Africa, the Olinkas thought Adam and Olivia were Nettie's and Samuel's children. They told Nettie the story about roofleaves:There had been a greedy chief who cut down much of the jungle in order to create more farmland. The plants, which provided the leaves for the roofs of the Olinkas' houses, were destroyed, and many people died. The village began worshipping the leaves. When Nettie looked at the roof of her new house in the village, she knew she was in front of the Olinkas' God.

Olinka girls were not educated. Olivia was the only girl at school. Corrine, jealous and worried by the Olinkas' impressions about her family, asked Nettie to tell the children not to call her Mama. Olivia's only girlfriend, Tashi, could not come to school because her parents forbade it.

After five years of silence, the next letter tells Celie that Adam and Olivia had discovered connections between slave stories and African stories. Tashi's father had died, and her mother had let her go to school. A road was now near the village, and suddenly the Olinkas realized it was going to destroy their sacred place. The chief went to the coast to do something about it, but he discovered that the Olinkas' whole territory now belonged to a rubber company.

When Corrine got ill shortly afterwards, she

told Nettie she thought Adam and Olivia were Nettie's and Samuel's kids. Though Nettie swore it was not so, Corrine was not convinced. Nettie and Samuel talked about it, and Samuel told her that Celie's and Nettie's real father was not the man they called "Pa"'; their mother had been married before to a man who was lynched by white people. In this way, Celie is freed from the nightmare of believing her children are also her brother and sister.

Fourth Period

For the first time, Celie writes a letter to Nettie. She has visited her old house with Shug and seen her Pa. Meanwhile, she goes on reading Nettie's letters.

Nettie and Samuel tried to convince Corrine of the real story of the children. She believed them only when Nettie made her remember meeting Celie in town. Corrine smiled to them then but died soon afterwards.

'I don't write to God no more, I write to you (Nettie)," says Celie in her next letter. She sees she has been praying to a *white* old *man*. Shug tells Celie she believes God is not a He or a *She*, but an *It*. It is everything, and It gets very angry if one walks by the color purple in a field and doesn't notice it.

Shug and Celie decide to leave Mr. together with Mary Agnes, who wants to be a singer. Celie curses Mr. and tells him that everything he did to her, he did to himself. The two women go to Shug's house in Memphis. Then, Shug travels around singing, and Celie starts Folkspants, Unlimited, a family clothing business.

When Celie goes back home to see Sofia and Harpo, she finds Mr. has changed. He cooks and cleans. Now they can talk. Harpo tells Celie his father could not sleep until he sent Celie the last letters he had kept.

The letters say Nettie and Samuel got married in the middle of the Olinka war. The company destroyed the roofleaves. Some of the Olinkas went to the jungle to search for the *mbeles*, a legendary tribe. Samuel and Nettie travelled to England and in the journey, Nettie told the children their real story. They were eager to meet Celie, but Adam missed Tashi. When they got back to Africa, the Olinkas were so desperate that they had marked their children's faces to keep their tradition alive. Tashi had the traditional scars in her cheeks.

In America, Celie's stepfather dies and she inherits the house. She cleans it of its horror with a ceremony and sells her pants there. Shug goes back to Memphis. Celie is very sad and lonely, and she then hears that the ship Nettie had taken to go home was sunk by the Germans.

But Nettie's letters keep arriving. Tashi, her mother, and Adam all disappeared from the village. Meanwhile, Mr. and Celie are united through heart-break and their love for Shug. Celie discovers that Mr. loves to sew. While they work together, she tells him the Olinkas' version of Adam and Eve's story: Adam and Eve were the first white babies in a black world, rejected because they were different. The serpent represents black people. Whites crush this serpent when they can because they are still enraged. In time, white people will be the new serpent and colored people will crush them. The only way to stop this horror is to worship the serpent and accept that it is our relative.

In her last letter, Nettie tells Celie that Adam and Tashi went to a secret valley where people from different tribes lived together. When they came back, Adam wanted to marry Tashi, but she rejected him. Adam scarred himself to convince her, and then they got married.

Sofia starts working in Celie's store. She is with Harpo again. Mr., who is now called Albert, asks Celie to marry him, but Celie prefers friendship. Shug comes back to them. Celie's last letter in the book is to God, but this time it is Shug's God. Celie is happy: Nettie, Samuel and the children are home at last.

Characters

Adam

Adam is Celie's son who was adopted by the missionary, Reverend Samuel, and his wife, Corrine. When the Reverend and his family return to America, Celie is reunited with her grown son.

Albert

Albert is the widower with four children who buys Celie from her stepfather. Albert treats Celie with cruelty, using her to satisfy his sexual needs and to take care of his children. He really loves Shug Avery, who later comes to live with Albert and Celie when she is sick. Celie appreciates Shug's presence in the house, because Albert treats her better when Shug is around. Albert later in life softens and Celie takes him in as a helper in her business.

Albert's father

Albert's father comes to visit when he hears that Albert has taken Shug Avery into his house. He says many nasty things about Shug and expresses his disapproval of what his son is doing. Albert asks him to leave.

Alphonso

Celie's stepfather. When Celie's mother is sick and dying, he rapes Celie and continues to do so long enough for Celie to have two children, whom he sells to a local missionary and his wife. He doesn't tell Celie what has happened to the children, and initially Celie thinks he killed them. Celie later learns that he is not her real father. Her real father was lynched years before by a white mob. Alphonso tells Celie not to tell anyone but God about what he has done to her. He warns her that if she tells, it will kill her mother.

Mary Agnes

See Squeak

Shug Avery

Shug, a blues singer, is the woman that Albert loves. She is a sophisticated and liberated woman. After she comes to stay with Albert and Celie, who care for her while she is sick, she and Celie develop a deep relationship. Shug helps Celie gain self-esteem and teaches her to speak up for herself. She finds the letters from Nettie to Celie that Albert has for years kept hidden away from Celie. Shug also helps Celie get started in her business by encouraging her to sew. Later in the story, Shug returns again to Celie and Albert's home, but this time with a husband. Along with Sofia and Nettie, Shug is a role model who helps Celie change her life.

Miss Beasley

See Addie Beasley

Addie Beasley

Nettie and Celie's teacher, who recognizes the girls' intense desire to learn. Their stepfather, Alphonso, is contemptuous of her when she tells him that his daughters are smart.

Carrie

Carrie is a sister of Albert's who comes to visit. She tells Celie that Celie is a much better housekeeper than Albert's first wife.

Celie

Celie is the heroine of the novel. Most of the letters that comprise the book are letters Celie writes to God or, after learning that her sister Nettie is in Africa, to Nettie. Celie does not know about Nettie's attempts to communicate with her until Shug finds the letters from Nettie that Albert has hidden. Through the character of Celie, the author is able to present her message of sexual liberation and self-determination for women. Through Celie's voice, which speaks in black folk English, life in the world of a poor, black, rural sharecropper family unfolds. In the beginning of the story, Celie is a young girl who has been raped by her stepfather, who later sells her to Albert, her husband. Both men treat Celie cruelly and without any regard for her needs or feelings. Celie is forbearing and a hard worker, for which every one praises her. When Albert's mistress, Shug, comes to live with them, Celie becomes liberated from her oppression because of Shug's intervention on her behalf, and because she learns to stand up for herself with Shug's encouragement.

Corrine

Corrine is the Reverend Samuel's wife. Corrine and Samuel are missionaries who adopt Celie's children. Nettie becomes their helper, and the missionaries leave for Africa with Nettie and the children. When Corrine dies in Africa, Nettie marries Samuel. She and Samuel, along with their adopted children, Adam and Olivia, return to America when war breaks out in Africa. Adam's African wife Tashi also comes to America with them.

Fonso

See Alphonso

Grady

Shug Avery's husband, whom she brings to meet Celie and Albert later in the story after some absence from Celie and Albert's home. Shug and

Media Adaptations

- Steven Spielberg directed and produced *The Color Purple* in 1985. The film starred Whoopi Goldberg as Celie, Oprah Winfrey as Sofia, Danny Glover as Albert, Margaret Avery as Shug Avery, and Willard Pugh as Harpo. While the film was nominated in every major category of the Academy Awards, it won no Oscars. It did, however, win awards from the Directors Guild of America, Golden Globes, and the National Board of Reviews. The film also helped launch the careers of Oprah Winfrey and Whoopi Goldberg. It is available as a home video by Warner and Facets

Multimedia.

Harpo

Albert's son. Harpo marries Sofia and they have five children. In his relationship with Sofia, Harpo tries to live up to his father's role as the domineering male. Because Sofia is a strong-willed young lady, she becomes disgusted with the way Harpo treats her and leaves him for a time. When she returns with a boyfriend, Harpo is jealous. Eventually, they get back together, but their relationship changes. Harpo accepts her strong character and stops trying to dominate her.

Warden Tom Hodges

The officer in charge of the prison where Sofia is sent after she insults the mayor's wife. When his niece, Squeak, comes to see him in an effort to get Sofia released from prison, Hodges rapes her. Walker uses this scene to illustrate the mentality of racism in the South during the period of the novel. Hodges is the brother of Squeak's white father. Because his niece is black on her mother's side, Hodges has no qualms about sexually assaulting her.

Queen Honeybee

See Shug Avery

Kate

One of Albert's sisters. On one of her visits she tells Albert to buy Celie some clothes.

Livia

See Olivia

Mama

Celie's mother, who is sickly and dies in the early part of the story. When she refuses to have sex with her husband, Albert, he rapes Celie.

Mammy

See Mama

Mayor

The mayor of the town with whom Sofia has a run-in. Sofia is jailed for insulting the mayor and his wife.

Miss Millie

See Millie

Millie

The mayor's wife, with whom Sofia has a runin. Sofia insults Millie and is arrested. After serving ing her sentence, Sofia is freed only to become the live-in caretaker of Millie's children.

Mr.

See Albert

Mr.'s daddy

See Albert's father

Nettlie

Celie's younger sister. Nettie is saved from a fate like Celie's because she has been taken in by the Reverend Samuel and his wife Corinne. When they leave for Africa on missionary work, Nettie goes with them. Nettie's letters to Celie are written in standard English to reflect the fact that she received a better education than Celie. In her letters to Celie, Nettie tells her a great deal about Africa, which comes to represent the larger world as well as African-American ethnic identity in the novel. When the Reverend's wife dies, Nettie marries him. She continues to raise his adopted children, who happen to be Celie's by her stepfather. Nettie returns to America and reunites Celie with her children.

Odessa

Sofia's sister. Odessa takes care of Sofia's children when Sofia is sent to jail.

Olivia

Celie's daughter by her stepfather. Olivia was adopted by the Reverend Samuel and his wife Corinne, along with her brother Adam, who was also one of Celie's children. Olivia returns to America with the Reverend, Nettie, Adam, and his wife, Tashi, and is reunited with Celie, her birth mother.

Old Mr.

See Albert's father

Pa

See Alphonso

Pauline

See Olivia

Prizefighter

When Sofia returns home after leaving Harpo for a substantial absence, she brings a prizefighter with her. He is her boyfriend, and Sofia uses him to make Harpo jealous.

Reverend Mr.

See Reverend Samuel

Reverend Samuel

The missionary who adopts Celie's children from Albert. Celie does not know they have been adopted. She thinks Albert killed them. The Reverend, his wife, and Nettie, who has been taken in by them, leave with the children for Africa to do some missionary work there. After the Reverend loses his wife, he marries Nettie.

Sofia

One of the three major female characters in the story who have a positive influence on Celie. Celie sees how Sofia stands up for herself to Harpo and to the white community as well. When Sofia becomes disgusted with Harpo's behavior toward her, she leaves him for awhile. When she returns, she taunts him with her new boyfriend, a prizefighter. Eventually, Sofia and Harpo reunite in a different relationship. When she is insulted by the mayor's wife, she talks back and causes a scene, for which she is arrested and thrown in jail.

Squeak

Squeak becomes Harpo's girlfriend after Sofia leaves him. When Sofia returns she is quite nasty to her, but she also helps Sofia out when she is jailed for standing up for herself from being insulted by whites. When Squeak intercedes for her with her white uncle, Warden Tom Hodges, she is raped by him.

Sugar

See Shug Avery

Swain

The musician who performs at the jukejoint Harpo has built.

Tashi

Adam's African wife, who comes to America with him and the rest of the missionary family when they flee Africa to escape hostilities there.

Tobias

Albert's brother, who comes to visit Shug while she is sick at Albert's house. He brings some chocolate, and they socialize while Celie teaches Shug to quilt.

Uncle Tom

See Warden Tom Hodges

Sexism

Sexual relations between men and women in *The Color Purple* is a major theme. Alice Walker sets her story of Celie's transformation from a passive female to an independent woman within the culture of southern black rural society from the 1920s to the 1940s. In the beginning of the story, Celie is dominated first by her father, whom she later learns is really her stepfather, then by her husband, Albert (Mr.). The catalyst for the character change in Celie is the relationship she develops with Shug Avery, her husband Albert's mistress. Because Celie has been warned by her stepfather, Alphonso, not to tell anyone but God about how he repeatedly rapes her, she begins to write letters to God. It is through the letters that the reader develops a sense of Celie's being, which at first is selfeffacing, but eventually becomes strong and independent.

In the novel there are a number of role reversals that take place between men and women. Harpo, Albert's son, tries to emulate his father and attempts to dominate his strong-willed wife, Sofia. By the end of the story, Harpo and Sofia have reversed traditional male-female roles. Harpo stays home to take care of the house, while Sofia works. Celie and Albert also reverse roles. By the end of the story, Celie is an independent businesswoman, and Albert is her assistant. Celie has also learned to speak up for herself, claiming her house when her stepfather dies. The sexual relationship between Celie and Shug further breaks with the traditional roles of passive women and dominant men that the story challenges. In the relationship between Samuel and Corrine, the missionaries who adopt Celie's children, and later between Nettie and Samuel, Walker presents what could be called a partnership relationship between a man and woman. In these relationships, both the man and the woman share the same goals and work together to realize them. Walker uses the incident between Squeak and her white uncle, the warden at Sofia's prison, to illustrate how sexism and racism were expressed. The warden has no qualms about raping his own niece, which reflects a southern, white, male disregard for the dignity of black women. During the period of the novel, it was a commonly held view among white males that they could do whatever they pleased with black women, a view that many black males shared as well.

Topics for Further Study

- Alice Walker has been criticized for portraying negative male characters in *The Color Purple.* Explain why you agree or disagree with this analysis. Be specific in your discussion by citing passages that support your viewpoint.

- Research the history of the epistolary novel and give three other examples of this form in literature. For each example, include the title, author, date of publication, and a summary of the novel. Many epistolary novels are written from the main female character's point of view. Are there any advantages or disadvantages to using this literary form when the major character is a woman?

- Research colonial rule in Africa. Narrow your scope by focusing on one European country and one African country that was colonized by it. Give a history of the African country before, during, and after European colonization.

- Sexual violence is a major theme in *The Color Purple*. From current media reports write an essay on how sexual violence is presented to the public. Include statistical information on sexual violence, such as the extent of increase or decrease in occurrences over the past 20 years. What are the underlying causes of sexual violence? Are there any methods for combating sexual violence that have been proven effective?

Transformation

Celie's transformation from a young passive girl, who is the object of violence and cruelty from her stepfather and her husband, into an independent woman with self-esteem is at the heart of *The Color Purple*. While the ways in which conflicts are resolved may stretch the imagination at times, they are central to the author's view that goodness can triumph over evil. That Celie is able to forgive Albert by the end of the story and take him in as a helper reflects Walker's insistence on the redeeming quality of the human heart. She shows in transformed relationships that the worst cruelty committed by one person on another does not prohibit a change of heart. Her view is basically that the conditions under which human beings struggle shape their behavior. Albert had a difficult life and took out his frustrations on Celie. When Celie became self-sufficient, she could easily have turned her back on Albert, but it is not within the framework of her character to be uncharitable. In becoming independent, Celie has found happiness. Rejecting Albert would detract from her happiness. Celie's behavior toward Albert reflects Walker's insistence on forgiveness and contributes to the overall religious overtones of the book.

Culture

Cultural difference plays a significant role in *The Color Purple.* Walker effectively uses black folk English in Celie's letters to express the voice of poor, black rural African Americans. Walker presents a clear picture in the book of the economic and social hardships that African Americans faced in the rural south during the early 1900s. She also presents an honest picture of the effects of racial repression. The picture Walker paints of black life is not one-sided. While Celie and Albert are tied to the land and the harsh life it represents, Nettie es-capes into a black middle-class life through her missionary friends. Religion in the South played an important role in liberating many African Americans from poverty. As a spin-off for involvement with the church, literacy and education flourished. Celie is embracing a religious literacy through her letters to God, and in her letters to Nettie she comes to grips with the larger world, including Africa, outside her small community. By making the connection to Africa, Walker emphasizes the importance of African Americans' roots.

Point of View

The Color Purple is written in the first person, and the voice is predominately Celie's, but some of the letters that comprise the book are written to Celie by her sister Nettie. The story covers thirty years of Celie's life from childhood to her maturity as an independent woman. By having Celie write in black folk English, Walker brings the reader close to the quality and rhythms of life that her characters experience. Celie's dialect also reflects her lack of formal education. Nettie, who was formally educated, writes her letters in standard English. They are full of information that becomes a source of knowledge for Celie outside the world of her own small community.

Structure

The structure of The Color Purple is the series of letters Celie writes to God and to her sister Nettie. Some of the letters in the book are written by Nettie to Celie. This literary form is called the epistolary novel, a form developed in eighteenth-century England by novelists like Samuel Richardson. A major advantage of this structure is that the reader becomes intimate with the character of the letter writer. With the epistolary form, Walker was able to focus on the inner life of her main character and create a sense of intimacy that may be partly responsible for the success of the book. This technique creates a confidential reading experience. The reader has a chance to read over the character's shoulder and look inside her. Nettie, to a great extent, escaped the cruelty that Celie experienced because she was able to leave home early. The tone of her letters to Celie contrasts sharply with Celie's letters to God. In Nettie's letters, there is much less intimacy. They do not contain the suffering that Celie has expressed in her letters to God. By introducing Nettie's letters, Walker is able to shift her story from Celie's life of despair to a life that begins to have hope. It is through the help of Shug Avery that Celie finds her hope—the letters from Nettie that Albert had hidden from her.

Basically there are four time frames of the novel. In the first period of her life, Celie experiences the misery of poverty and cruelty at the hands of her stepfather. In the second closely-related period, Celie experiences continued cruelty from her husband Albert. In the third period, she awakens to the possibility of self-realization through her relationship with Shug and her renewed contact with her sister Nettie. Finally, Celie has realized herself and has established a life where she has control; she has found the happiness and contentment that come from self-realization. Another period, not directly a part of Celie's life, is Nettie's time spent in Africa. The letters from Nettie serve as a contrast to Celie's life. They also enlarge Celie's perspective and help to universalize her life.

Symbolism

The primary symbol of *The Color Purple* is found in the title, *The Color Purple.* The significance of the color purple is that it stands for human hope. It is a miraculous color, when found in nature, and one which indicates that the feeling of hope, despite misery, is a miracle of the human spirit.

Black-White Relations in the Rural South

After slavery, the social and economic relations for African Americans remained much the same. While no longer slaves, many blacks remained on the land as sharecroppers. They tilled the soil, but the land was owned by their former slave masters. After 1915, economic opportunities in cities of the industrial North encouraged many blacks to leave the South. Those that remained continued to live isolated from white society. Schools and churches were segregated, as well as housing. There were few opportunities for blacks to establish themselves outside of sharecropping. During the period of the novel, segregation between blacks and whites was enforced legally to the point that blacks had to sit in separate parts of movie houses and drink out of separate fountains, and were forbidden from eating at white lunch counters. The laws that were passed to enforce this segregation were called Jim Crow laws, named after a pre-Civil War minstrel character. In *The Color Purple* Sofia is victimized by this social policy. When she shows defiance to the white mayor's wife who insults her, she is arrested and given a stiff jail sentence for her actions. The difficulty in relations between black men and women had its source in white male-dominated society. Within white society, men were expected to control the family and had status over women. This attitude filtered into black culture, but the black male, unlike his white counterpart, was humiliated daily for the color of his skin. In frustration, many black males turned their anger towards women. Black women then experienced the double oppression that Alice Walker explores in the novel.

Lynching, murder by a mob, was prevalent in the South from the 1880s to the 1930s. Celie's real father had been lynched in the 1900s because he had established a business that competed with white businesses. White southern businessmen felt economically threatened when a black business took black customers from them. Retaliation by lynching went unchallenged until the United States Congress tried to pass an anti-lynching law in 1937. Southern senators killed the bill by not letting it come to a vote in the Senate.

African-American Religion

In their letters, Celie and Nettie talk about God. Celie confesses that she sees God as white, but Nettie replies that being in Africa has made her see God differently. Her African experience has made her see God spiritually rather than in the physical form that is represented in Western Christianity. While most African Americans were either Baptist or Methodist during the first half of the twentieth century, the way they expressed their religion in church was much different from white congregations. Infused into the services were elements from their African roots, particularly a distinct musical style and delivery of the sermon in a moving manner. The congregation answered the preacher at key points in the service, and singing was accompanied with expressive physical movements, like clapping and swaying. The main reason that African Americans were drawn to the Baptists and Methodist churches was that these two denominations had opposed slavery early in American history. By the late eighteenth century, blacks were forming congregations within these Protestant sects. In 1816 religious leaders from the black community met in Philadelphia and established the African Methodist Episcopal Church (AME), which still has sizable congregations throughout the United States.

Compare & Contrast

- **1930s:** The relationship between men and women is clearly defined. Men are the bread-winners and the heads of the families. Women stay at home to take care of the children and the housework.

  Today: Men and women share the economic burden of the household. Many married women with children are in the workplace. Preschool children are cared for in daycare centers or at home with paid baby-sitters.

- **1930s:** Racism is condoned throughout the country, and laws in the South enforce segregation. African Americans are kept out of many industries.

  Today: Discrimination on the basis of race, gender, ethnicity, or disability in the workplace is illegal.

- **1930s:** Violence against women is widespread and ignored by the police.

  Today: Violence against women is illegal, and perpetrators are being vigorously prosecuted in both civilian and military life.

- **1930s:** Most religious African Americans belong to either a Baptist or Methodist congregation.

  Today: Many African Americans have turned away from Christianity to the Muslim religion. Strong leadership has developed within the Black Muslim movement to keep it a viable religious alternative for African Americans.

- **1930s:** Colonialism dominates the African continent. It is carved up among the major nations of Europe who exploit it for its rich resources.

Today: All nations in Africa are self-governed, but the remnants of colonial mismanagement have led to unrest in a number of African countries.

Critical Overview

Since its publication, *The Color Purple* has aroused critics to both praise and to sharply criticize elements in the book. Trudier Harris in *Black American Literature Forum* criticizes the media for dictating the tastes of the reading public. The book "has been canonized," she states. It has "become *the* classic novel by a black woman," because "the pendulum determining focus on black writers had swung in their favor ... and Alice Walker had been waiting in the wings of the feminist movement...." Harris contends that the popularity of the book has been harmful because it has created "spectator readers," and it "reinforces racist stereotypes." Because of the book's popularity, Harris maintains that black women critics are particularly reluctant to find fault with the book, even when they find elements in it disturbing. She also questions the novel's morality, which other critics praise. "What kind of morality is it that espouses that all human degradation is justified if the individual somehow survives all the tortures and ugliness heaped upon her?" The morality other critics find in *The Color Purple*, Harris feels "resurrect[s] old myths about black women." This critic cites Celie's response to her abuse as an example of the myth of submissiveness of black women. She also criticizes the sections dealing with Nettie and Africa because she feels they "were really extraneous to the central concerns of the novel" and accuses Walker of including them "more for the exhibition of a certain kind of knowledge than for the good of the work." The relationship between Celie and Shug, Harris also felt, was silly. Another criticism Harris has of the book is what she considered its fairy tale element. "Celie becomes the ugly duckling who will eventually be redeemed through suffering," says Harris. The book, she feels, "affirms passivity … affirms silence … affirms secrecy concerning violence and violation … affirms … the myth of the American Dream.…" Anyone can achieve "a piece of that great American pie." Harris accuses the author of preparing "a political shopping list of all the IOUs Walker felt that it was time to repay." In spite of her sharp criticism of *The Color Purple*, Harris confesses that she is "caught in a love/hate relationship with" it.

Surprisingly, one of the most positive reviewers of the book was Richard Wesley. Writing in *Ms.* magazine, Wesley says "As an African-American male, I found little that was offensive as far as the images of black men," as they were portrayed in the book and the film. In his review, Wesley sees the character of Mr. emblematic of "male privilege. As long as black men seek to imitate the power structure that crushes them … and as long as black women submit … then the morbid relationship of Celie, the oppressed, and Mr., the oppressed oppressor, will continue to be played out in homes all across America." In his article, Wesley criticizes those who fault *The Color Purple* for painting a negative image of black males. "Walker is airing dirty linen in public. She is reminding many of us men of our own failures. She is reminding women of *their* failures as well.... A lot of people do not want to hear that." His strong support of the novel concludes his review. "No one in America—and black America, especially—should be telling writers what they may or may not say. Writers are the antennae of any society. They have to speak when others dare not." Another male writer, J. Charles Washington, writes in *Obsidian* that Walker is justified in concentrating on female characters, who have been neglected by male writers. It "does not mean that she is anti-male," he says, "but that she has less time and energy to devote to exploring more fully the problems of men or the common causes of the oppression of both...."

Also writing in *Ms.*, Gloria Steinem finds much to praise and little to criticize in Walker's novel. "... white women, and women of diverse ethnic backgrounds, also feel tied to Alice Walker. The struggle to have work and minds of our own, vulnerability, our debt to our mothers, the price of childbirth, friendships among women, the problem of loving men who regard us as less than themselves ... are major themes" of Walker's writings. "She speaks the female experience more powerfully for being able to pursue it across boundaries of race and class," Steinem maintains. She finds the author's storytelling style "irresistible to read." Countering Trudier Harris's criticism, Steinem feels pleasure in "watching people redeem themselves and grow." Its symbolism of purple, Steinem notes, represents "the miracle of human possibilities."

Sources

Trudier Harris, "On *The Color Purple*, Stereotypes, and Silence," in *Black American Literature Forum*, vol. 18, no. 4, 1984, pp. 155-61.

Gloria Steinem, "Do You Know This Woman? She Knows You: A Profile of Alice Walker," in Ms., June, 1982, pp. 35, 37, 89-94.

J. Charles Washington, "Positive Black Male Images in Alice Walker's Fiction," in *Obsidian*, Spring, 1988, pp. 23-48.

Richard Wesley, *"The Color Purple* Debate: Reading between the Lines," in *Ms.*, September, 1986, pp. 62, 90-2.

For Further Study

Richard Abcarian, *Negro American Literature*, Wadworth, California, 1970.

> An early but fundamental commentary on African American literature, its roots and importance. There is a deep discussion of Richard Wright's novel.

Gordon W. Allport, *The Nature of Prejudice*, Cambridge, 1954.

> An early, fundamental source to understand the problem of prejudice, and racism in general, and to help define concepts such as visibility and difference.

Barbara Christian, editor, *Black Feminist Criticism*, Pergamon Texto, University of California Press, 1985.

> A number of essays about black literature from the feminist criticism perspective.

Arthur Davis and Michael W. Peplow, *Anthology of Negro American Literature*, Holt, New York, 1975.

> A collection of critical essays on early African American literature.

Leslie Fiedler, "Negro and Jew: Encounter in America", in *No! In Thunder*, Stein and Day, New

York, 1972.

> An interesting article by a very well-known critic about the relationships between Jews and African Americans in the United States.

Paula Giddings, *When and Where I Enter: The Impact of Black Women on Race and Power in America*, Bantam, 1985, p. 186.

> Giddings, a historian, discusses the role of color and its impact on achievement. She offers supporting evidence that African Americans of mixed race (with lighter skin color) had better educational and economic opportunities than those with dark skin color.

Nathan Glazer and Daniel P. Moynihan, editors. *Ethnicity: Theory and Experience*, Harvard University Press, Cambridge, MA, 1975.

> A study of the relationships between "Self" and "Other," written after some important observations of the sixties.

Jacquelyn Grant, "Womanist Theology: Black Woman's Experience as a Source for Doing Theology," in *Encyclopedia of African American Religions*, Garland, 1993, p. 1.

> Grant explains the concept of *womanist* as opposed *to feminist.* A distinction in terminology is made

for black women because their struggle for expression has been different from white women.

Bell Hooks, *Ain't I Woman: Black Women and Feminism*, South End, 1981.

Hooks discusses the sexual assault black women endured after the end of slavery and the passive role of black women after World War II.

Charles Frederick Marden and Gladys Meyer, *Minorities in American Society*, Van Nostrand, New York, 1973.

An early study of ethnic relationships in the United States. The most detailed section of the book is devoted to the problems faced by African Americans in the United States.

S. Dale McLemore, *Racial and Ethnic Relations in America*, Allyn and Bacon, Boston, 1980.

A much more advanced study of the subject of ethnic relations in the United States with a big section devoted to African Americans and a deep discussion of cultural versus racial differences and visibility.

Toni Morrison, *Playing in the Dark, Whiteness and the Literary Imagination*, Picador, 1992.

The essential, interesting ideas of Nobel Prize winner Toni Morrison about African American literature, its roots, purposes and future.

Carol Pearson and Katherine Pope, *The Female Hero in American and British Literature*, Bowker, New York, 1981.

> An essential study of women in literature that is very interesting for understanding the position of Celie as heroine in *The Color Purple.*

Annis Pratt, *Archetypal Patterns in Women's Fiction*, Indiana University Press, Indiana, 1981.

> This study can be applied to the use of archetypes and myth in *The Color Purple.*

Elaine Showalter, *Towards a Feminist Poetics*, Oxford, 1979.

> A study about feminist poetic theory, with interesting ideas that are applicable to *The Color Purple.*

Claudia Tate, *Black Women Writers at Work*, Continuum, New York, 1983.

> A series of interviews with black female authors, including one with Alice Walker. The interviews have a distinctively feminist focus, making them especially interesting to anyone studying *The Color Purple.*

Fannie Barrier Williams, in Paula Giddings's book, *When and Where I Enter: The Impact of Black*

Women on Race and Power in America, Bantam, 1985, p. 114.

> Williams discusses the historical attitude of black men toward black women, an attitude that devalued black women and assumed they were not virtuous.

Lightning Source UK Ltd.
Milton Keynes UK
UKHW020807010822
406672UK00010B/1208

9 781375 398077